CW00958641

From Fleece ᵥ ...

The Technological History of the
Welsh Woollen Industry

J. Geraint Jenkins

(Curator Welsh Industrial and Maritime Museum Cardiff)

Gomer Press
1981

First Impression—September 1981
Second Impression—October 1987

ISBN 0 85088 785 2

Printed by J. D. Lewis & Sons Ltd.
Gomer Press, Llandysul, Dyfed

1. Introduction

Sheep have always been the mainstay of the economy of many parts of rural Wales and the fact that the country supported such extensive flocks of sheep accounts in no small measure for the wide distribution of the Woollen Industry in the Principality. Many of the mills of rural Wales were entirely dependent on processing wool obtained from farms in the immediate locality of the mill and the carding and spinning equipment within those mills was designed specifically for processing the short-stapled wool of Welsh mountain sheep. Many of the mills were concerned merely with providing a service for local farmers; wool was brought to the mill together with the order for knitting yarn, blankets or flannel by the farmers for their family needs. In many cases the mill owners kept a proportion of the fleeces that a farmer brought in; perhaps a tenth and this represented the farmer's payment for processing the wool. Under this semi-barter system, no cash payment of any kind was involved and the cloth made from the surplus was sold by the mill owner on the open market and represented the cash profit from his activities.

Not all mills were dependent on supplying farmers with their day to day necessities and neither were they all dependent on local wool. Large mills in early nineteenth century Powys and early twentieth century Teifiside, for example, were entirely dependent on wool merchants for their raw materials, but whether the wool was local or foreign the mill owner had to pay the merchant in cash. Some of the mills, especially before shearing time obtained 'skin wool' or 'pulled wool' from fellmongers; the wool being obtained from sheep slaughtered for mutton. The fellmongers obtained wool either by soaking pelts in water, hanging them in ovens and then pulling the wool or by painting the inside of the pelts with sodium or lime. The latter method of fellmongery produces the so-called *slipe-wool*, favoured until recently by many Welsh manufacturers. Many Welsh mills in the past, however, did not deal with fellmongers or wool merchants and preferred to deal directly with the farmer. Sometimes they paid partly in cash and partly in goods, but the wool they purchased after shearing time in June and July was expected to last the year.

Since the formation of the British Wool Marketing Board in

1950, Welsh textile manufacturers have to a great extent lost their connection with local growers and merchants; indeed since the foundation of the Board it has been illegal for woollen manufacturers to buy their raw material directly from the farmers. Slipe wool may still be obtained from the fellmongers, but to many, wool that has been subjected to chemical treatment is regarded as being harsher and inferior to shorn wool. The Wool Marketing Board is responsible for selling and distributing all the fleece wool produced in Britain and few Welsh manufacturers have ever attended the annual wool sales at Bradford or Leicester. Most of them depended on wool factors who purchased fleece wool on their behalf and it was most unlikely that the wool obtained contained more than a small proportion of wool from Welsh sheep. In any case, no more than three mills in the whole of Wales today process wool from fleece to fabric, for the majority purchase skeins of dyed and spun yarn from Yorkshire manufacturers. Most Welsh mills today are weaving factories that do not practise the intricacies of sorting, willeying, carding and spinning; indeed even the finishing processes are transferred to Yorkshire manufacturers, for the process of milling and nap raising are now alien to many a Welsh factory owner. Many of the processes described in this volume are no longer practised in the majority of the woollen mills of Wales.

2. Wool Sorting

The sorting of wool in a mill is one of the most skilled of all textile processes and in the past many a factory owner undertook this task himself or passed the work exclusively to the most experienced and skilled worker in his mill. Even in the larger mills of Powys and Dyfed in the late nineteenth and early twentieth centuries, the wool sorter was always the most highly paid employee of the mill. In some districts, especially Newtown and Llanidloes in the early nineteenth century, the manufacturers depended on specialised wool staplers for their raw material, while in recent times wool obtained from fellmongers and wool merchants may already be sorted into grades before it ever arrives at a factory.

4

Tom Griffiths, sorting wool, 1940

Wool varies tremendously from sheep breed to sheep breed, but there are also variations in different sections of a fleece. Hence, the better quality wool from the shoulders and sides has to be separated from the short, often dirty wool of the tail, belly and legs. If a fleece were used without sorting, the resulting yarn would be faulty and uneven and dyeing would be patchy. If a fleece is not properly sorted, a cloth woven from it would be very poorly finished, for the finishing processes depend very much on the felting qualities of wool and those qualities may vary very much in different parts of a fleece.

It is the farmer's duty at shearing time to ensure that the fleece is properly folded. Fleeces are always folded in three lengthwise and are tied with a band made by pulling out the neck wool, twisting it and winding it around the folded fleece.

The wool sorter has to unfold the fleece on a well-lit table and begin the task of 'skirting' it; that is, removing the inferior belly wool. The equipment used by the wool sorter is not extensive. He needs a pair of shears for cutting and a table or sorting board placed in such a position that a good light, usually a 'north light' is always available. The bale of wool is usually placed on the left of the sorter while on the right are placed three or four skips into which the various qualities of wool are sorted. Discoloured wool, paint, dirt and vegetable matter may be placed in another skip or in a box. The sorting board is partly made of slats so that dust and other impurities fall through the slats to the floor below.

The method of grouping wool may vary tremendously from mill to mill. But in the main, the following are the main criteria adopted by the most skilled of wool sorters:-

1. The appearance and condition of a fleece and the softness and harshness of wool when handled.
2. The length of staple,—that is, the unstretched measurement of a fibre from tip to base.
3. The degree of lustre,—the gloss or sheen.
4. The degree of springiness,—that is the extent to which a handful of wool will expand after being compressed and then released.
5. Colour,—the nearness to black or white.
6. Strength of fibre,—'sound fibre' (that is strong) or 'tender fibre' (that is easily broken).
7. Degree of fineness,—this is referred to by quality number —100s, 90s, 50s, 40s, 32s, etc., the higher number referring to fine wools, the lower to the thickest, coarsest fibres. Originally, these numbers referred directly to the thickness or 'count' of yarn it was possible to spin from the wool, but gradually this correlation has been lost and there is no connection between wool quality and yarn count.

Bearing all these complex criteria in mind, it is obvious that wool sorting is not a task for a novice and it is work that can only be undertaken after many years' experience. Categories of wool depend very much on the individual's judgement. A mill in Dyfed, for example, classified its wool into four categories:-

6

1. Best white for white yarn.
2. Second best for dyeing into lighter pastel shades.
3. Light grey used without dyeing or for producing dark shades.
4. Dark grey for dyeing into black or brown.

Another mill in Gwynedd produced the following grades:-

1. Diamond,—best quality from shoulders, sides and backs of fleece for best tweed and flannel.
2. Pick,— Wool from belly used for tweed and flannel.
3. Super,— Coarse wool, but even fibred for blankets and rough flannel.
4. Middle,— Coarse wool used for horse blankets and for stuffing horse collars.
5. Britch,— Wool from legs and neck used for making floor coverings and the rougher type of cloth.

A large mill in the Teifi valley in the nineteen twenties produced nine grades of wool based on the classification in Yorkshire mills. They were,—

1. Super diamond,—the best quality from the shoulders.
2. Extra diamond,— from the sides.
3. Diamond,— from the back.
4. Neck (or shafty)—short, fine fibres.
5. Picklock,— belly wool, often felted.
6. Prime britch,— coarse, long staples from haunches.
7. Britch,— coarse and dirty from hind legs.
8. Brokes,— poor wool from fore legs
9. Pole lock,— coarse, straight fibres from the head.

Today, of course, the limited quantities of fleece wool purchased by Welsh Woollen manufacturers has to be purchased through the Wool Marketing Board who have special categories that number 16 for Welsh fleeces.

3. Willeying

Willeying is a process carried out on wools that are heavy with dust and sand and is aimed to disentangle the fibres of wool before carding and, in some cases, before scouring. By willeying, it is maintained that less soap is necessary. For the last 150 years or so, willeying has been a mechanical process where a water-driven machine that resembles a barn thresher is employed. This machine, that contains a large revolving toothed roller, is known by a variety of names—'willey', 'willow', 'teaser', 'wool mill', 'twilley', 'diafol' and 'diawl'. Before wool is passed through the willey, vegetable oil at the rate of two pints to fifteen pounds of wool is evenly sprinkled on the wool on the feed table at the front of the machine, and as this is drawn rapidly into the body of the willey, oil and wool are thoroughly mixed. Of course, oiling of wool is necessary to facilitate the carding process.

The water-driven willey became common in most Welsh mills after about 1820, but before then, willeying was a hand process. A quantity of wool was placed on a horizontal hurdle or a series of cords fixed to a rectangular framework and beaten with wooden rods. It is said that these rods were made of flexible willow, hence the term 'willowing' or 'willeying' for the process of beating wool.

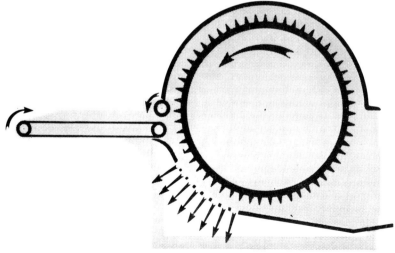

The mechanism of a willey used for the disentangling of wool

4. Scouring

In most Welsh woollen mills, except the larger, wool was proc-
essed in the grease without any preliminary washing or
scouring. Many believed that all impurities would have been
washed away when sheep were washed before shearing. It was
also believed that, for flannel and blankets in particular, a far
closer weave could be ultimately obtained if unscoured wool
was used. To most manufacturers, it was the finished product,
be it blanket or a length of cloth, that had to be scoured and
dried; not the raw wool.

Nevertheless, in a few of the larger mills wool was scoured;
the most common method being to immerse raw wool in a
solution consisting of one part human urine to three parts
water. The practice of collecting urine in a cask from the
homes of a textile producing district was commonplace for not
only was it used for scouring, but also in fulling and dyeing. Of
course, wool immersed in scouring solution had to be thoroughly cleansed in running water before it could be used.
Usually, the wool was placed in a large basket anchored by
rope to the banks of a stream or mill-race, so that the wool was
thoroughly rinsed.

Large coopered tubs with perforated false bottoms were also
used for scouring. Soda ash and soap were the cleansing agents
and the impurities in the wool dropped through the perfor-
ations in the bottom of the tub. Quite often in the mills of
Dyfed, soap, either for scouring wool or washing fabrics, was
made by burning bracken and mixing the resulting ash with
water.

A few of the larger mills of the early twentieth century installed standardised scouring machines made by a Rochdale
machinery manufacturer. The first automatic scouring
machine was patented by John Petrie of Rochdale in 1853 and
the firm of Petrie and McNaught still remain the leading
manufacturers of scouring machinery in the country. The
usual method of mechanical scouring is in a series of four
troughs or bowls where wool passes successively through four
bowls; each having a lower temperature and a lower concen-
tration of detergent than the previous one. A series of power-
driven forks transfer the wool from one bowl to the next.

Wool will soon deteriorate if it is left in a damp state and it is necessary to dry it thoroughly before it can be used. In the past, small batches of scoured wool were dried in the sun, but some of the larger mills installed drying racks. Here, wool was spread out on a wire mesh table under which were steam pipes. In some cases fans were installed to increase the circulation of hot air.

5. Dyeing

The stage in production at which wool is dyed varies according to the preferences of the textile worker and the type of cloth to be woven. In some cases raw wool, sometimes scoured, sometimes in the grease is dyed before carding. In the past, this was done in large, open vats and the worker would stir the boiling dye and wool at frequent intervals with a pole. In the smaller rural factories, this method of dyeing still persists. At the Esgair Moel Mill from Llanwrtyd in Brecknockshire, now at the Welsh Folk Museum, for example, the usual method is to dye unwashed raw wool in a large 30-gallon copper vat. The dye vat is always heated with wood fires and there is a tradition in Brecknock that the best timber for heating purposes is alder, which up to 1939 could be obtained from the itinerant clog sole makers who frequently visited the alder groves of the county and sold waste timber locally. The practice of dyeing raw wool in the grease has a distinct disadvantage in that the rollers of the carding engines have to be cleaned at frequent intervals, to ensure that one colour does not contaminate another. This is particularly true where white wool follows a strongly coloured one through the carding set; indeed, some of the larger late nineteenth century woollen mills in west Carmarthenshire installed two carding sets; the one for white wool, the other for coloured wool.

Nevertheless, where cloth of a mottled or mixed colour is required, it is essential to dye wool in the raw state, so that the colours are thoroughly intermixed in the blending or willowing process.

As an alternative to dyeing the raw wool, the fibres may be dyed at the yarn stage, either in the form of hanks suspended from rods or in the form of packages known as 'cheeses' or 'cones'. These packages consist of a pound of yarn wound on bobbins and immersed in a dyeing vat. Since there is no movement of the yarn in the dyeing the wool does not become felted as in the other processes. Cheese dyeing is preferred in cases where fine yarn is required.

A great many woollen cloths are dyed in piece form; that is, as lengths of woven cloth. In many mills a wooden winch with a cranked handle is fixed above the dye vat and this was used for rolling the dyed cloth from the vat below. In the eighteenth century, the flannel of mid-Wales, if it was to be coloured at all, was usually piece dyed by the dyers employed by the Drapers' Company of Shrewsbury.

Wool is a highly reactive substance and no difficulty is experienced in bringing about combination with dyes. The art of dyeing goes back to prehistoric times and natural dyes such as woad, indigo and wortle-berries were well-known to ancient civilisations. Before synthetic dyes were available, the first one was discovered in 1856, textile manufacturers throughout the world were dependent on natural dyes. They depended on a great variety of vegetable dyes such as madder, foxgloves and lichens together with different metallic mordants such as iron, alum and tin. With these natural dyes, the range of colours was extremely limited and considerable variation and unevenness could exist where the vegetable matter was harvested at different times of the year. Colour could also vary considerably according to the length of time the wool was boiled in the dyeing liquid. For example, if the wool was boiled with birch leaves for three-quarters of an hour, it would produce a pale, yellow colour. If it was boiled for a further half hour, the wool would take on a distinctly green colour. On the whole, the colours produced by vegetable dyes on their own were rather dull and lifeless. Very often too the methods of mixing dyes depended as much on guesswork as on recipes passed down over many generations. Although synthetic dyes became increasingly available in the eighteen-sixties and eighteen-seventies only the larger mills of West Wales had taken advantage of them by the end of the century. Most of the smaller mills clung to traditional methods of dyeing and during the first decade of the present century, textile manufacturers on sending out patterns of cloth specified the method of dyeing. A pattern book of textiles made at the Tonypandy Mill in Glamorgan in 1912, for example, shows tweeds at 3s 6d a yard

11

—a red 'dyed with madder', a purple 'dyed with black berry', a blue and white 'dyed with indigo' and shades of green 'dyed with indigo ground with fustic'.

Natural dyes are divided into two distinct classes:-

a) SUBSTANTIVE or NON-MORDANT DYES, which impart their colour directly to the wool on immersion and boiling.

b) ADJECTIVE or MORDANT DYES, where wool has to receive special preparation before it can absorb colour. The process of preparing is called 'mordanting' and the four mordants used in the Welsh woollen industry were:

    i) *Alum*—A salt dissolved in water at the rate of one part alum to four parts water. Wool was boiled in this for an hour, allowed to cool and then washed in soapy water.

    ii) *Chrome*—(Bichromate of Potash)—Added at the rate of half an ounce to a pound of wool.

    iii) *Tin* (Stannous Chloride)—Used in the same way as chrome.

    iv) *Copperas* (Ferrous Sulphate Copperas)—Added at the rate of 5 ounces to 100 pounds of wool. Wool was dyed first and then boiled for half an hour in the copperas. Copperas was obtained from a blacksmith's shop, in the form of water that had been used for cooling iron or it could be obtained by boiling rusty iron in a dye vat. In some parts, mountain streams contain iron to make mordanting a very simple process.

A wide variety of colours could be obtained from simple raw materials. The quantity of dye included in the vat, the length of boiling and the time of year when the plants were picked could all affect the final colour of wool. Birch leaves, for example, were best used in the early spring. If fresh leaves were used then the weight of leaves should have been equal to the weight of wool. On the other hand, if the dyer used dried leaves then he would need four times the weight of wool to be dyed. The leaves had to be soaked for twenty four hours and the wool boiled in the solution for no more than an hour. This would produce a yellow wool, but if boiling were to go on for a longer period, the wool would turn green. If the birch dyed wool was mordanted with alum, the resultant colour would be a bright yellow, chrome mordanting would produce tan and iron or copperas mordanting, a blackish brown. In general, the longer wool was boiled, the darker it became. The following are some examples of the colours produced by dyers in Wales to the end of the nineteenth century. There were, of course, countless variations in colour, some of them demanding the admixture of numerous elements and many hours of preparation. These examples, however, represent some of the simpler types of recipes with one or possibly two dyeing agents boiled with the wool.

Dark Brown
Yellow wall lichen; red currants (with alum); crottle; bracken (with chrome or alum); privet (with copperas); sorrel (on its own or with chrome, alum or copperas); walnut shells; dock (with alum or copperas); blaeberry (with gall nuts).

Tans and Light Browns
Lichens (on their own or with alum, chrome or tin); sloe berries; elderberry; birch leaves (with chrome); broom flowers (with copperas); bracken; weld (with copperas); privet (with chrome); bedstraw (with chrome); onion skin; heather (with chrome).

Blues
Blaeberry (with copperas); elder (with alum); indigo; woad.

Black
The most popular method was to boil copperas with gall nuts, oak bark or sawdust.

Greens
Gorse; privet berries (with salt); iris leaf; broom; heather (with indigo); unripe blackthorn; birch leaves. It was very difficult to obtain a good green colour, and more often than not wool was dyed blue and then yellow or vice versa.

Purples
Blaeberry (with alum); bitter vetch; blackberry.

Yellows

Leaves of apple, ash, buckthorn, hazel, birch (with alum); bracken root; St. John's wort; rock lichen; dog's mercury; gorse; weld (on its own or if darker colours were required, with tin, chrome or alum); privet (with alum); heather (with alum); bedstraw (with alum); nettles (with alum).

Orange

Ragweed; bramble.

Magenta

Dandelion.

Reds

Bedstraw roots; madder; tormentil roots; foxgloves; cochineal; lichens (with ammonia).

Principal Dyes Used in the Welsh Woollen Industry— Eighteenth and Nineteenth Century

Cochineal

Obtained from insects in south and central America and imported. Used on its own it produced a rather dull, uninspired pink, but with tin mordant the colour became a very fast, bright scarlet. Other colours produced were purple (with chrome mordant), crimson (with alum mordant), and lilac (with iron mordant).

Kermes

Also obtained from insects and used to dye red.

Nutgalls

Used as a basis for preparing a number of colours, mainly blacks and greys. Nutgalls helped the wool to take the dye and make it fast.

Madder

This was cultivated in many parts of Britain and was valuable for dyeing red, cinnamon and brown. The roots alone were used for dyeing and harvesting of plants, at least four years old, took place in the autumn months. Pounded madder boiled with alum and cream of tartar produced red that was fast, but not as bright as that dyed with cochineal.

Old Fustic

A species of mulberry. The logs of a deep sulphur colour were widely used by Welsh dyers. Main colours—yellow, green and olive. By using sumac with it, the colours became far more permanent.

Young Fustic

The wood of Venetian sumac. Chips of wood were steeped in water and the solution when boiled with wool produced a variety of colours ranging from yellow, through orange to green.

Weld

The 'dyer's rocket' grows best on chalk soils. The whole plant except the roots was used and the best quality was autumn cut, second year plants. Boiled for three-quarters of an hour on its own, weld would produce a pale yellow colour. If mordanted wool was used, many shades of yellow and light brown could be obtained. A very fast colour.

Turmeric

This plant root, though occasionally used by dyers produced a bright yellow which soon faded. Occasionally it was used to give an orange tint to scarlet.

Woad

Harvested in summer and ground into a paste at a woad mill and dried. On its own it produced a permanent though dull blue.

Indigo

An important plant widely used for dyeing colours ranging from crimson to light blue. Known as 'blue ynde' or 'dents dye'. Had to be pounded before use, and in some cases dissolved in oil of vitriol. Synthetic indigo is still used in the modern textile industry to give very fast dark blue or navy blue colours.

Verdigris

Produced by rubbing vegetable acids, such as plums or grapes on copper and used in conjunction with other dyes for dyeing black.

Cream of Tartar

Obtained from the bottom of wine casks after fermenting and used in conjunction with a large number of other elements for dyeing a variety of colours, mainly for assisting fixing. Also used with alum to prevent it crystallising on woollens.

Alder Bark

Ground alder bark used with alum or copperas produced a dark brown colour.

Lichens

Produced very fast dyes. Equal quantities of wool and lichen were boiled for at least an hour. The longer the boiling, the deeper the colour became. The type of lichen also affected the colour. To produce a pale green for example, rock moss (cen du y cerrig) was boiled for an hour and a half, while tree lichen boiled for the same length of time produced a tan colour. Colour could also vary according to whether the lichens were picked in dry or damp weather.

Sloe

One pound of well-bruised berries added to a pound of wool and boiled for two hours, produced a rose colour. If the wool was washed immediately in soapy water, the wool turned into a slaty green.

Elderberry

Bruised berries boiled with an equal quantity of wool produced a brown yarn. A bluey-green was produced after mordanting in alum. Elder-dyed wool was said to fade very badly in sunlight.

Dog's Mercury

Added at the rate of two parts dye to one part weight of wool. Produced a pale yellow after an hour's boiling.

Hazel Leaves

Two parts hazel to one part weight of wool, boiled for slightly less than an hour produced light brown.

Privet

One and a half parts dye to one part wool to produce light green that was not very fast. The addition of chrome produced light brown and copperas produced a dark brown.

Sorrel

Sorrel roots added at the rate of two parts to one part wool and boiled for three or four hours produced a brown.

Bedstraw

One of the few plants that produced red. Equal quantities of bedstraw root and wool, boiled for two hours gave brown; if chrome was added, it produced a yellowy-green. If the bedstraw flowers were used and boiled for at least an hour, with the addition of chrome or alum, the colour produced was a rather lifeless pinky-red.

Gorse

Bark, flowers and young shoots added to an equal weight of wool and boiled for a maximum of an hour, produce a yellow. Could also be used as a yellow mordant.

Broom

Best collected in April and added to an equal weight of wool, boiled slowly for an hour to produce a moss green.

Bracken

Picked in May or June and added to wool at the rate of two parts to one part wool, simmered for an hour to produce brown.

Heather

A good fast dye if young flowers were used. Tops were placed in cold water, brought to the boil and allowed to cool for four hours. The liquor was strained and added to wool to boil for an hour. The colour produced was a browny-yellow.

Nettle

The leaves and stalks were soaked in cold water for twenty-four hours. The wool was boiled in the liquor for two hours to produce a drab, yellowy-green colour.

Dock

Roots were pounded and soaked in water for twenty-four hours. Boiling with alum for two hours produced a darkish brown.

Onion Skin

Boiled with an equal quantity of wool to produce an orange-yellow, that was not very fast.

Walnut

Shells were placed in a cask of water, and the longer they were kept the darker the colour of wool became. After boiling for half an hour, a dark brown was produced. Also added to indigo for producing black.

Buckthorn

Unripe buckthorn berries were crushed in water, and the infusion evaporated to the consistency of honey. After boiling the wool in this, a green colour could be obtained.

Other raw materials found occasionally in recipes of the eighteenth and nineteenth century were saffron (crocus corms), safflower, annatto fruit, brasil wood and logwood.

Since the beginning of the present century, synthetic dyes have become increasingly more important in the Welsh woollen industry. Today, the woollen manufacturer can obtain hundreds of synthetic dyes, covering the whole range of the visible spectrum.

6. Carding

According to the most proficient weavers, a key to the quality of finished cloth is the nature of the yarn and this itself is dependant on the process of carding. If the carder does not perform his work efficiently, then one can not expect the finished cloth to be of high quality. One of the main reasons why the Welsh woollen industry declined in the nineteen twenties was the poor quality of yarn due to the inefficiency of the obsolete carding equipment found in many mills. 'The very sight of some of the carding engines', said W. P. Crankshaw in 1927, 'is enough to drive any well trained carder to commit suicide'. After all, a spinning jenny will produce yarn just as well as the most modern ring spinner, a hand-loom will produce cloth as good as that produced on a modern automatic loom, but should the carding equipment be in poor condition then the efforts of the spinner and weaver would all be in vain.

Carding is the process of opening out the fibres of wool to produce a fully disentangled, soft roll of wool ready for spinning. The thick threads produced by the carder are called a

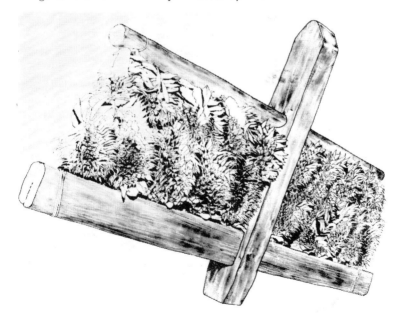

A teasel card used for carding wool before wire brushing

slubbing or *roving*. The word carding is derived from the Latin *cardus* (thistle); thistle heads having been used in antiquity for the process of disentangling wool. In Wales, however, the earliest method of carding was to place prickly teasel heads in a rectangular hand frame and use the frames in pairs to produce rovings. So important was the teasel plant that its Welsh name was *llysiau'r cribwr* (the carder's plant) and teasel gardens were found in many parts of the Principality. Nevertheless since the fourteenth century the most common method of carding was to use hand cards. Each card consisted of a wooden board about 9 inches long and 6 inches wide with a wooden handle. One surface of the board is covered with leather penetrated by thousands of small metal teeth. The maze of teeth was known as *card brushing*. Hand cards were always used in pairs. A small quantity of wool was placed on one card and pulled gently apart with the teeth of the other card. After a time the wool became evenly distributed among the teeth of the two cards.

A hand card

One card was then moved in the reverse direction and the loosened fibre collected together, in the form of a short spongy sliver. Before spinning, the rolls of wool had to be fixed together to produce a continuous, long roll. This process was known as *piecening*.

Although hand cards were used in Wales until the end of the nineteenth century, carding benches were also known in Powys in the eighteenth century. In this, card brushing was tacked to a sloping board and the operator armed with one card only sat on a bench attached to the bench. Wool was spread evenly on the fixed card and removed with the hand card.

20

Various other hand devices were tried in the eighteenth century but the most ingenious of all pieces of equipment was the carding engine; a piece of equipment that is still used in the modern textile industry. 'Undoubtedly the woollen carding machine (carding engine or card)' said one author 'is a fascinating and wonderful one . . . It was one of the pinnacles even among all the wonderful achievements of the age of mechanisation'.

It was Daniel Bourn, a Leicester cotton manufacturer who thought of the idea of attaching card brushes to cylinders which could be turned by hand. His patent of 1748 was not succesful. Lewis Paul, a shroud maker in the same year invented a machine in which a cylinder covered with card brushing rotated against another stationary cylinder. This machine too was no great success and it was left to the famous Richard Arkwright to produce an usable machine that was based on Bourn's and Paul's patents. Between 1775 and 1782, Arkwright patented a number of machines and important innovations were brought in. His carders were equipped with fluted feed rollers which drew the wool into the machine, and a series of rollers that turned almost in contact with a large central roller. It was similar to the mechanism of the modern carding engine, found in woollen mills the world over. By 1780, Sir Richard Arkwright's carding engines were well known in West Riding mills and within twenty years water driven machines were well-known in the flannel manufacturing districts of Powys. The design of the carding engine was said to have been smuggled into Wales from Yorkshire by a John Jarman.

The carding engine really consists of two machines—the *scribbler* responsible for the initial disentangling of wool and the *carder* itself responsible, with fine card brushing, for producing the slubbing. Scribbling machines vary in size and a scribbler at a modern mill may consist of two or three separate machines joined to one another. The simplest type, as found in the Esgair Moel woollen mill at the Welsh Folk Museum, has a large central cylinder called a *swift* covered with coarse brushing. A number of smaller rollers also covered with brushing revolve, nearly in contact with the swift. The larger ones called the *workers* revolve fairly slowly and the smaller, faster revolving rollers are known as *strippers* or *cleaners*. To card wool, the raw material is spread evenly on the slowly rev-

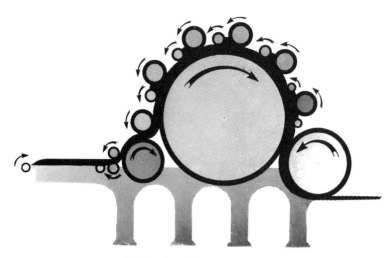

Mechanism of scribbler carder

olving *feed table* at the front of the machine. A pair of revolving *feed rollers* draw the wool into the body of the machine to a large roller known as the *licker in* or *breast roller*. After being thoroughly carded by the action of workers and strippers the wool reaches a large, rapidly revolving roller at the back of the machine, known as the *fly* or *fancy*. The wool is removed from the swift to be passed on to the slowly revolving *doffer*. In turn the wool is stripped off the doffer by a steel comb that moves rapidly up and down to provide a long roll of wool—the *roving* or *slubbing*. Nowadays, mechanical *intermediate feeds* transfer the

Mechanism of the carding engine

roving from scribbler to carder, but before 1866 the scribbled wool had to be removed from the scribbler by hand and transferred to the feed table of the carding machine proper. This machine with its arrangement of workers and strippers revolving around a central swift is the same as the scribbler, except that a final roller with some form of rubbing mechanism condensed the carded wool into thin, soft rovings ready for spinning.

7. Spinning

The slivers of wool that come off the carding engine or hand cards are very soft, thick and easily broken. They can not be used for weaving cloth until they are made much stronger by stretching and twisting. The process of converting carded slivers into strong yarn is known as *spinning*.

Distaff spinning

In prehistoric times and indeed until the close of the Middle Ages, spinning was done with a spindle and whorl. The equipment for this was extremely simple and consisted of a piece of wood, often elaborately carved on which a bundle of wool was placed. This was known as a *distaff*. A strand of wool was taken from the bundle and attached to a piece of wood, perhaps 12 inches long—the *spindle*—which was weighted at the bottom with a perforated stone weight—the *whorl*. The wool was paid out by hand and the spindle rotated by hand, with the whorl acting as a weight to maintain spin. After a length of wool had been converted into yarn, it was wound on to the spindle and the process repeated. Very fine yarn could be produced by the *distaff* spinners and in parts of Eastern Europe the equipment is still used by women to produce yarn, especially of fine linen. They often undertake spinning while shepherding, for the great advantage of the spindle and whorl over other methods of spinning is not only the fineness of thread that can be produced, but also the portability of spinning equipment. In some parts of Gwynedd, the spindle and whorl was still used for producing fine yarn in the mid-nineteenth century.

A great revolutionary change took place in the Welsh woollen trade in the fourteenth century for among the important devices that appeared during that century, one of the most important was the *Great Wheel* for spinning. This was not such a portable piece of equipment as the spindle and whorl and very soon the spinning wheel became an essential part of the furnishing of many a country home. It never demanded such a high degree of expertise and judgement as the older method of hand spinning and the ability to spin on a wheel came to be regarded as an essential qualification for many women. The very word 'spinster' undoubtedly relates to the process for spinning, unlike weaving, was never carried out by men.

Most women stood for the spinning process. The wheel was revolved with the right hand and with it revolved the spindle in the centre. A little wool was attached to the spindle, drawn back with the left hand for about five or six feet and twisted. When it was judged that a length of yarn was sufficiently twisted it was wound on to the cop on the spindle. The process was repeated until a cone of fully spun yarn was produced. Spinning required considerable dexterity,—it was a slow, tedious process that brought in very low returns to those engaged in it, yet the great wheel remained the principal piece of equipment in the Welsh woollen industry until more sophisticated, mechanised factory equipment became common during the second decade of the nineteenth century. It is true that attempts were made to improve hand spinning equipment,—the most important being the adoption of small treadle wheels, known in Wales as 'Anglesey Wheels', probably in the

24

'The great wheel'—the traditional Welsh spinning wheel

fifteenth century. This failed to oust the traditional great wheel and one had to wait until the late eighteenth century for a break-through in textile technology with the patenting of James Hargreaves' *spinning jenny* in 1770. In Wales, this was not an immediate success for great wheels could be produced by any country wheelwright; they could be bought for as little as five shillings and no special building was required to house them. Jennies did come to Montgomeryshire between 1795 and 1805 and since they were large machines, they had to be accommodated in special factory buildings, often alongside the carding engines that were already gaining in importance.

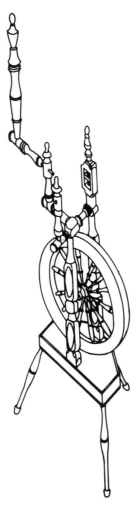

The upright 'Highland' spinning wheel that became popular in Wales in the nineteenth century

Hargreaves' spinning jenny spun twenty or more yarns simultaneously; it was a hand-operated machine and the process of drawing out wool and twisting it into thread was performed by a moveable clasp or clove that moved along the fixed top rail of the machine.

Although a large number of jennies were bought by Welsh factory owners, especially in Powys, by far the most important textile invention of the late eighteenth century as far as Wales

26

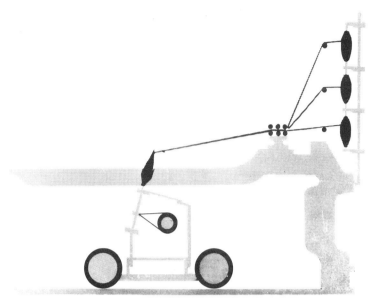

The working parts of a self-acting mule for spinning

was concerned was that of Samuel Crompton's mule of 1774. This was the machine that remained the backbone of the Welsh textile industry until quite recently; indeed some are still used in Welsh mills. Unlike the jenny, the carriage that carried the spindles in a mule was moveable along a pair of fixed rails and spinning was undertaken by drawing the carriage back and causing the spindles to turn either by hand, water or electric power. Early hand mules could have about 60 spindles but large, fully automatic mules could have as many as a thousand spindles turning simultaneously. The self-acting mule was the invention of a Powys engineer, Richard Roberts of Llanymynech (1789-1860) who made such a contribution to nineteenth century technology.

The late eighteenth and early nineteenth centuries was a period of great revolutionary changes in textile technology. In 1790, yarn required by weavers was produced by hand spinning; one spinster produced one thread. By 1835, despite the objection of many a spinster, a mule could produce hundreds of threads and usually one machine could be tended by one person. Ring spinning, so popular in the West Riding worsted industry, did not become popular in Wales, although

27

one mill installed this highly automated method of spinning in recent years. In most Welsh mills today however, no yarn spinning of any kind is carried out and mill-owners are largely dependent on specialised yarn manufacturers in West Yorkshire.

8.   Preparing Weaving Threads

Winding, unwinding and winding on again are processes always present in the stages of preparing yarn for weaving. Yarns from the spinning wheel or mule are skeined and usually the wool is stored in skein form. For weaving, the skeins have to be wound onto spools or cones for making the warp of cloth and wound onto shorter pieces of wood known as *pirns* or *bobbins* that will fit into the shuttle of a weaving loom.

Cloth is made up of longitudinal threads—the *warp chain*, intersected by transverse threads known as the *woof, weft, pick* or *filling*. Cones or spools for the warp are prepared on a winder or *swift* and since the warp threads have to be considerably tougher than the weft threads, it used to be common practice to size them. The size was usually made by boiling rabbit skins in water. For some thick cloths like the traditional *carthenni* or bed-covers, three-ply yarn may be required and this is produced by unwinding the thread from the cones by wheel or twisting machine. For lighter flannels, however, single ply yarn is thick enough.

Weft threads need not be as strong as the warp threads and they are wound onto bobbins that are not too thick to fit into the centre of a shuttle. By far the easiest method of doing this in the past was to place a bobbin in the centre of a spinning wheel and draw the thread from a hank of wool on a winder. Of course, in most mills today, power driven weft winders and warp winders with a multiplicity of spindles are in common use.

9.   Warping

One of the most intricate and complex of all processes in textile manufacture is the preparation of the warp; the threads that run lengthwise in the loom. All the threads have to be placed in

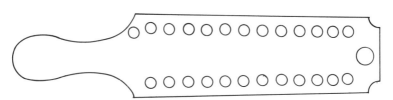

Warping bat used for arranging the warp threads on the wooden pegs

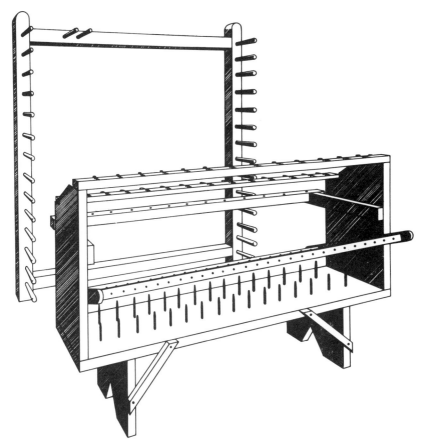

The traditional warping equipment. The creel at the front carried
the cops of yarn and the warping was completed on the wall pegs

the correct order with the correct colour sequence before weaving can proceed. Although today most mills have warping mills, the traditional method of preparing the warp was to arrange it carefully on the wooden pegs of a warping frame placed along the wall of the building. At the Esgair Moel mill a rectangular frame 88 inches by 77 inches carries 32 wooden pegs. It is between these removable and adjustable pegs that the warping is carried out. Parallel to the warping frame is a creel that carries the cops of wool. These cops are in two lines, the one in front of the other and they are carefully arranged in the creel according to the pattern and colour of the desired warp. The threads are passed through metal eyelets at the tope of the creel and through holes in the wooden warping bat held in the craftsman's right hand. This is used for placing the threads in the right position in between the pegs. Starting on the left-hand side at the top of the frame, the threads are stretched over and below the wooden pegs in the correct order from left to right and back again until the desired length of warp has been completed. This has then to be transferred to the loom, a process known as *beaming* or *looming*.

In the more modern warping mill, the creel carries a large number of cops and the work of the pegs in a more primitive set-up is carried out by a very large revolving drum. The threads are transferred automatically from the drum to a wooden beam that can be installed directly in a power loom.

10. Weaving

The process of weaving is that of interlacing the threads of the weft in between the threads of the warp. In all looms the warp is inserted first and the weft is completed by throwing a shuttle *(gwennol)* that carries the weft thread in between the warp threads. The threads of the warp have to be opened to provide a space or *shed* so that the shuttle can travel in between them to complete a row. As a length of cloth is completed it is necessary to have some battering or beating mechanism to make the cloth firm and compact.

By far the simplest type of loom is the warp-weighted loom, used throughout Europe in the Middle Ages. In this, the threads of the warp are tied to the top beam of an upright, rectangular wooden frame and kept taut by tying stones or lead

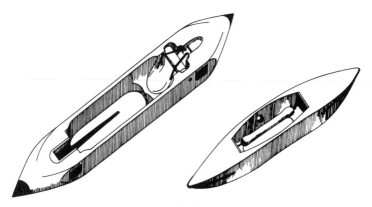

Loom shuttles
Left: Flying shuttle; *Right:* 'Banana' shuttle for hand looms.

weights to the bottom of each thread. The cloth was completed by passing a shuttle carrying weft threads in and out between the upright warp threads.

By the end of the Middle Ages, however, the hand loom with its pedals had taken over from the warp-weighted loom. The warp was now attached to a *warp roller* at the back of the loom and each thread was tied at the other end to a *winding roller* or a *cloth roller*. In the middle, and in front of the operator each thread was passed between the *heddles*, a series of vertical threads on wires. Each set of heddles, perhaps 300 or more in number were inserted in a rectangular frame, known as a *leaf*. Each leaf, and there could be three or four in an ordinary hand loom was connected to one of the front pedals. To raise the heddles and consequently the warp threads, one of the pedals was pressed so that the leaf was lifted and the shuttle could be shot across the warp in the shed provided. As the work proceeded the weft thread was beaten and packed close. The process is continued until a long length had been rolled on the cloth beam. Throughout the eighteenth century, from 1733 when John Kay invented the flying shuttle, great attempts were made by dozens of inventors to devise a power loom. Ox power, horse power, water power, and finally steam power were all utilised in an attempt to make the slow laborious hand weaving processes more efficient. In 1822, the Welsh inventor, Richard Roberts, of Llanymynech, Powys, devised a power loom, based on the original design of William Horrocks of

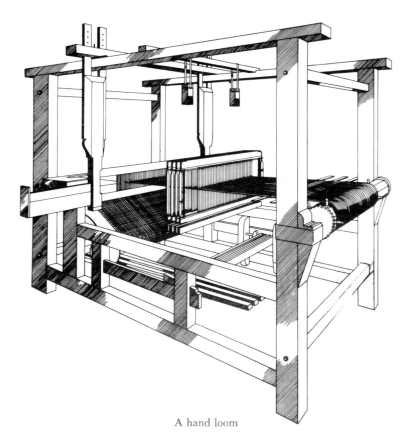

A hand loom

Stockport, that became a model widely used by manufacturers throughout Britain. The Welsh woollen manufacturers were not too ready to accept these new inventions for it was not until after 1860 that the power looms began to oust the traditional hand loom in Welsh weaving establishments.

The Jacquard loom for producing intricate patterns of flowers and other intricate non-geometrical designs never became popular in Wales and most of the designs are traditionally geometrical ones. The simplest form of weaving, known as plain or tabby weave, is that made by interlacing the warp with the weft, alternating over and under as in simple basketry. The cloth produced, and this may be seen in flannel still produced by Welsh mills today, has exactly the same appearance on both sides. Texture, of course, can vary by using heavier threads for the warp. In twill weave the threads are

Hand-loom weaving at the Esgair Moel Mill, Welsh Folk Museum. The weaver is Glyn Bowen.

Weaving a 'tapestry' quilt, Tregwynt Mill, St. Nicholas, Dyfed

interlaced so that the warp passes under two and over two warp threads to produce a diagonal or herringbone pattern. The multicoloured double-woven tapestry cloth, so often associated with Wales is really two cloths woven on the loom at the same time so that the pattern is completely reversible. Despite its association with the Welsh woollen industry in the present century, 'the tapestry' is as well known in Scotland, Kentucky, Eastern Canada and China as it is in Wales.

11. Fulling

Fulling is the process of shrinking and thickening cloth after weaving. In the Middle Ages, this was done by placing a length of cloth in a stream and walking over it with bare feet. In tne fourteenth century, water driven mills consisting of heavy hammers that beat up the cloth, became commonplace in many parts of Wales. These were the *Pandai* (singular *Pandy*), and the name *Pandy* in present day place names (for example Tonypandy) indicates the location of an early fulling mill.

Fulling cloth

A fulling mill consists of a pair of heavy wooden mallets lifted with wooden tappet wheels so that the hammers descend with some force on the cloth placed in the trough underneath. In the traditional process, cloth was fulled three times—with human urine, fullers earth and soap. The cloth was then washed in clean water and stretched out in the open air for drying on the *tenter frames*. The cloth was attached to the frame by the sharp *tenter hooks*.

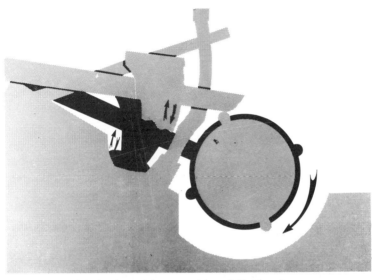

Mechanism of the water driven fulling stocks

Of course, light flannels and the lighter variety of tweeds and cloths produced by Welsh mills in recent years did not need the heavy fulling process and it was enough to wash cloth and mill it gently in a scouring trough. Soda was mixed with the water and there was a frequent change of water so that all traces of grease and oil were removed. Today, fulling is undertaken in a rotary wooden milling machine with revolving paddles to agitate the water within it. A hydro-extractor; an industrial version of a spin-dryer is often found in many factories to complete the milling process on cloth.

Tentering cloth

12. Napping

In processing certain types of fabric, especially blankets that
were produced by many Welsh mills until about 1960, it was
essential that the nap of the cloth was raised to give the blanket a soft, fluffy appearance. To do this a plant—the teasel
(llysiau'r cribwr) was widely used. There were many teasel
gardens in Wales, although the main source of supply was
Somerset. The teasel heads, usually harvested in the late
summer or early autumn, were inserted into a wooden bat and
the nap was raised by combing the surface of the blanket that
was fitted to a rectangual wooden framework.

The *gig mill* was a development from the hand teaseler.
Hundreds of teasel heads were fixed to a large revolving drum,
somewhat like a carding engine. The gig was driven by water
power and the cloth was moistened and brought gently into
contact with the revolving teasels so as to raise the nap.

36

In the past, some cloths were shorn after napping, the shearers using large shears to complete the work. This was highly skilled work and the cloth produced was described as 'dress finished'. By the mid-nineteenth century a water-driven cropping machine with revolving cutters was well-known in many Welsh mills. It is said that the original lawn mower was based on the design of a wool cropping machine, seen by its inventor in a Stroud woollen mill.